GW00384988

THE BRISTOL HISTORY
PICTURE AND QUIZ BOOK

- THIS IS A FUN BOOK FOR ANYBODY BETWEEN 8 AND 80. YOU CAN COLOUR IT WITH FELT TIPS OR COLOURED PENCILS OR PAINTS.
SOMETIMES A COLOUR SCHEME HAS BEEN SUGGESTED BUT YOU CAN USE YOUR OWN. IF IT IS A PICTURE OF SOMETHING THAT CAN STILL BE VISITED, FIND IT AND USE THE ACTUAL COLOURS.

- YOU CAN FILL IN THE MISSING WORDS IN BLOCK CAPITALS.

- IF YOU CANNOT ANSWER THE QUESTIONS, LOOK THEM UP AT THE BACK OF THE BOOK.

- AT ALL TIMES MAKE SURE THAT THIS BOOK IS:

SHIP SHAPE AND BRISTOL FASHION

REDCLIFFE
Bristol

BRISTOL IN VICTORIAN

SHIPPING. IN THE CENTRE FACTORIES, WAREHOUSES

INTO NARROW STREETS. FACTORY CHIMNEYS MINGL

SKYLINE. WHICH CHURCHES CAN YOU IDENTIFY?

S⁺ P_____

S⁺ J_____

S⁺ M _____

C _____

S⁺ P____ & S⁺ J_____

A _____

S⁺ N _____

S⁺ W_____

S

C _____ S _____

F _____

CENTRE OF BRISTOL FROM St MICHAEL'S HILL c. 1870.

St Philip & St Jacob. St Thom
St Mary Redcliffe. St Mary's
St Nicholas. Christmas Step
Which famous city churches

...IES WAS A THRIVING PORT CRAMMED WITH

...OPS AND POOR INSANITARY HOMES WERE PACKED

...WITH MEDIAEVAL CHURCH TOWERS DOMINATED THE

S^t M _____

S^t S _____

S^t M _____

F _____ H _____

...rtyr. St Peter's. Foster's Almshouses. St John's on the Gate. Christ Church.

...y. St Mary le Port. St Stephen's on the Quay. St Werburgh's. All Saints.

... Harbour. Temple Church.

...ible in this drawing? _____

Princess Victoria in Bristol 1830

Victoria first came to Bristol with her mother the Duchess of Kent, when she was 11 years old.

They stayed in the Clifton Hotel, in the Mall, which had been built as the Clifton Spa Assembly Rooms in 1806.

What places in Bristol are named after Victoria? _____

_____

_____

_____

The Architect, Francis Greenway was later arrested for fraud & transported to a convict settlement in Australia. There he was allowed to continue his career — and was acclaimed the Father of Australian Colonial Architecture.

THE VICTORIA ROOMS 1839

BEGUN 2 YEARS AFTER VICTORIA BECAME QUEEN.

1. In what style was it built? _____

2. Whose statue now stands in front? _____

QUEEN VICTORIA'S
NEXT OFFICIAL VISIT
TO BRISTOL WAS
IN 1899.

3. Where is this statue?

_____

4. Which war does this
   statue commemorate?

_____

5. Where is it?

_____

BRISTOL'S FAMOUS

CAN YOU IDENTIFY THEM?

1843

Name _____

Street _____

Style of Architecture

_____

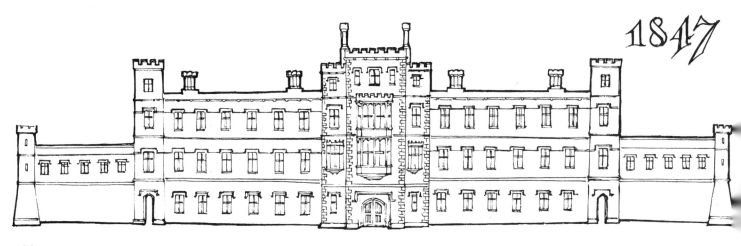

1847

Name _____

Situation _____

Style of Architecture _____

1857

Name _____

Style of Architecture

_____

How has it been altered

since 1857? _____

_____

_____

VICTORIAN BUILDINGS

Name _____

Street _____

Style of Architecture

_____

How has it been altered since

1858? _____

_____

1858

1871

1866

Name _____

Style of Architecture

_____

Name _____

Style of Architecture _____

How has it been altered since 1866? _____

1867

1894

Name _____

Style of Architecture _____

Name _____

Style of Architecture _____

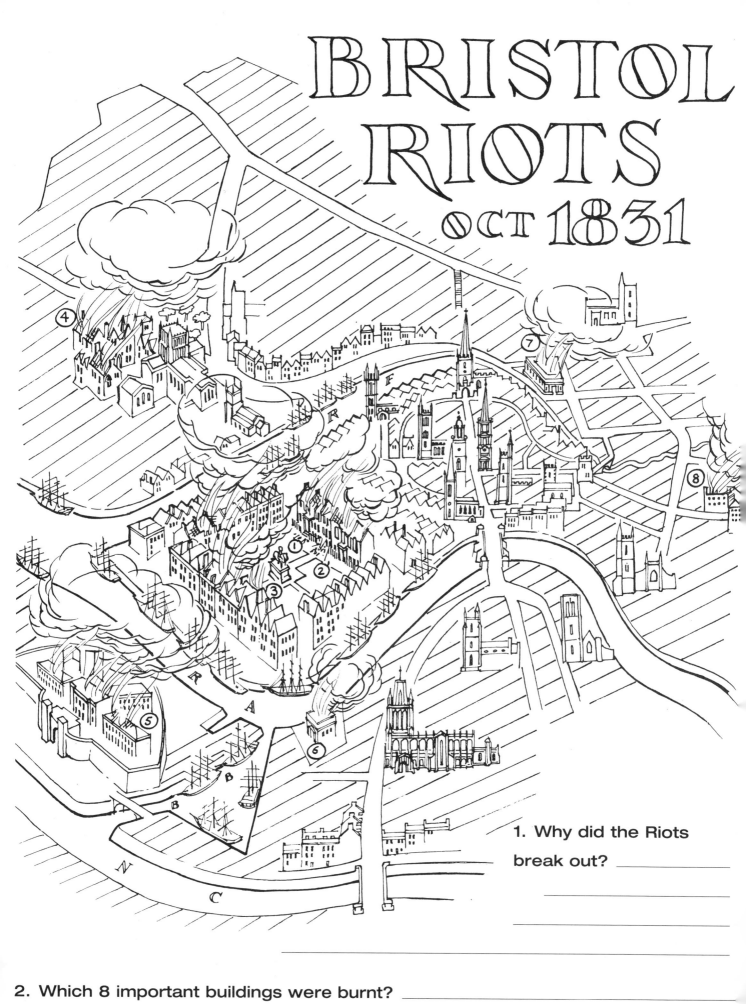

BRISTOL RIOTS

OCT 1831

1. Why did the Riots
break out? _____

_____

_____

_____

2. Which 8 important buildings were burnt? _____

_____

Colour shaded area of the City grey, fires red & yellow, church towers & rivers red (reflecting the fires). Label RIVER AVON, RIVER FROME, NEW CUT, BATHURST BASIN.

QUEEN SQUARE THE NIGHT OF 30 OCT: 1831

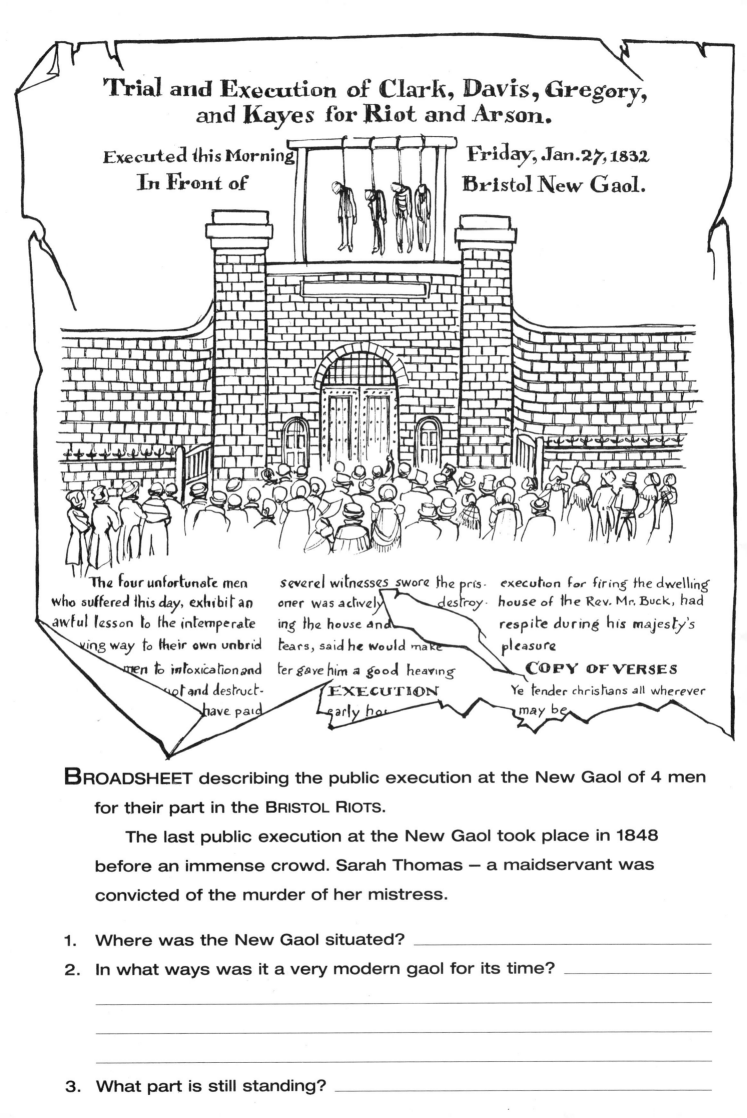

Trial and Execution of Clark, Davis, Gregory, and Kayes for Riot and Arson.

Executed this Morning
In Front of

Friday, Jan. 27, 1832
Bristol New Gaol.

The four unfortunate men who suffered this day, exhibit an awful lesson to the intemperate ...ving way to their own unbrid ...men to intoxication and ...ot and destruct- ...have paid

severel witnesses swore the pris- oner was actively ...ing the house and ...tears, said he would make ...ter gave him a good hearing

EXECUTION ...early ho...

execution for firing the dwelling house of the Rev. Mr. Buck, had respite during his majesty's pleasure

destroy-

COPY OF VERSES
Ye tender christians all wherever may be.

BROADSHEET describing the public execution at the New Gaol of 4 men for their part in the BRISTOL RIOTS.

The last public execution at the New Gaol took place in 1848 before an immense crowd. Sarah Thomas — a maidservant was convicted of the murder of her mistress.

1. Where was the New Gaol situated? _____

2. In what ways was it a very modern gaol for its time? _____

_____

_____

_____

3. What part is still standing? _____

BRISTOL'S FIRST POLICE STATION 1836

ON BRANDON HILL
Three others
were built at the
same time — in
Wine Street, St.
Philip's & the
Causeway
Bedminster, but
this is the only one
to have survived.

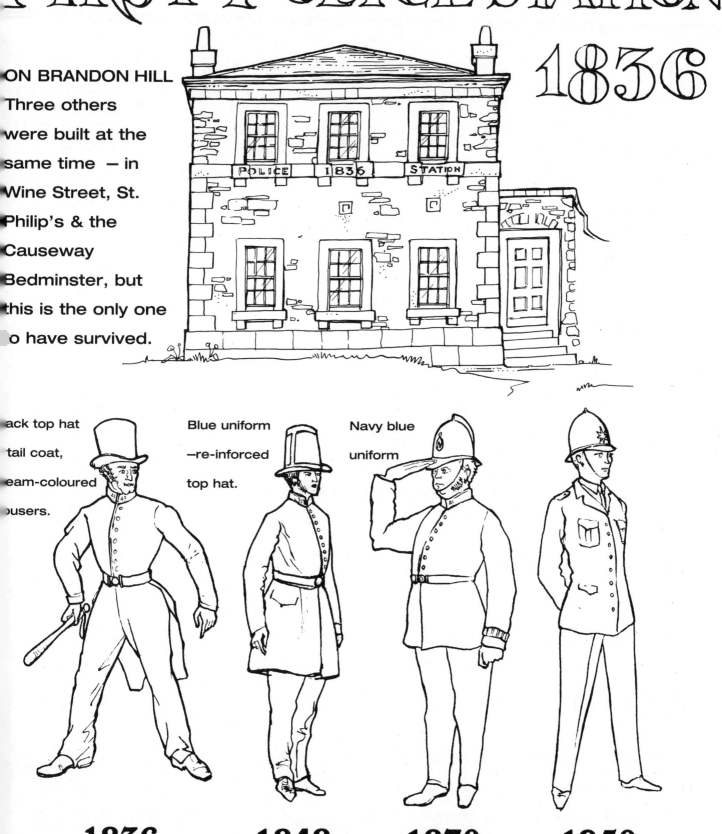

Black top hat
tail coat,
cream-coloured
trousers.

Blue uniform
—re-inforced
top hat.

Navy blue
uniform

1836   **1848**   **1870**   **1950**

ISAMBARD KINGDOM
BRUNEL
IN
BRISTOL

HE CAME TO CLIFTON IN **1828** TO RECOVER HIS HEALTH AFTER NEARLY BEING DROWNED WHEN SUPERVISING THE BORING OF THE THAMES TUNNEL BUILT BY HIS FATHER.

1830 HE WON THE COMPETITION FOR THE BUILDING OF THE CLIFTON BRIDGE.

1833 HE BECAME ENGINEER TO THE G.W.R. WHICH BUILT THE RAILWAY BETWEEN BRISTOL & LONDON.

1837 HE BUILT THE GREAT WESTERN STEAM SHIP.

1839 HE BUILT THE ROYAL WESTERN HOTEL – NOW BRUNEL HOUSE.

1843 HE BUILT THE GREAT BRITAIN STEAM SHIP.

Fill in the area above marked x x x in black and leave the rest white – & you will have a striking silhouette of Brunel. Where is the statue on the right? _____

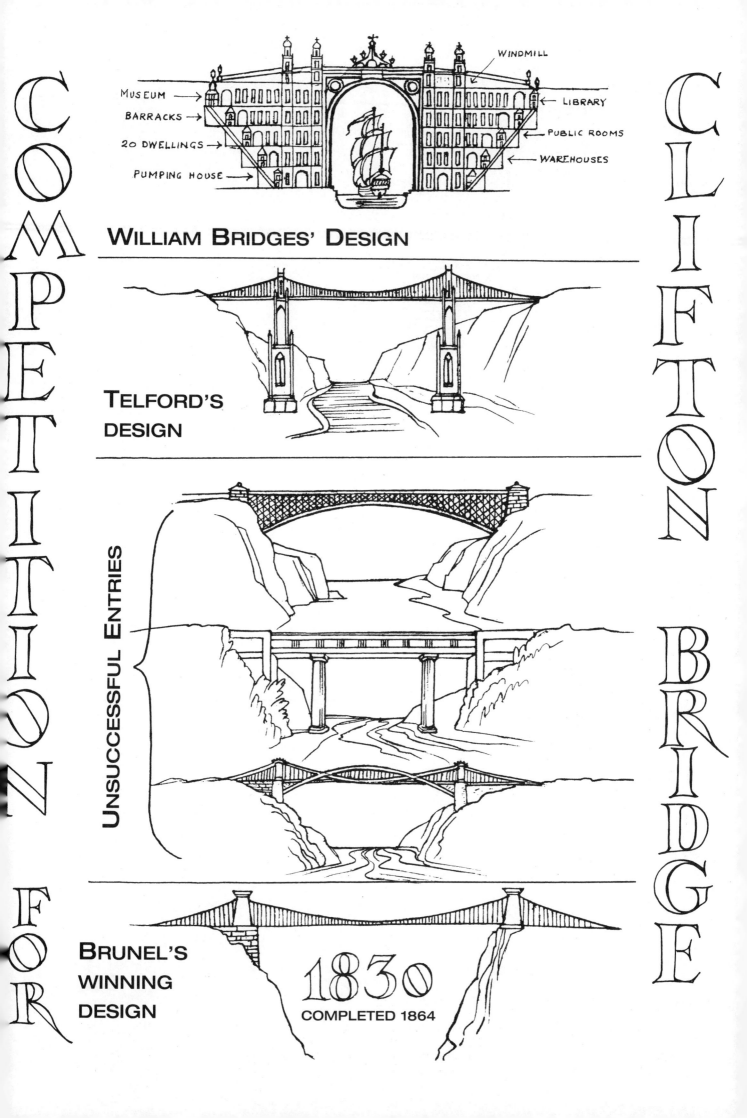

COMPETITION FOR

CLIFTON BRIDGE

MUSEUM
BARRACKS
20 DWELLINGS
PUMPING HOUSE

WINDMILL
LIBRARY
PUBLIC ROOMS
WAREHOUSES

WILLIAM BRIDGES' DESIGN

TELFORD'S DESIGN

UNSUCCESSFUL ENTRIES

BRUNEL'S WINNING DESIGN

1830

COMPLETED 1864

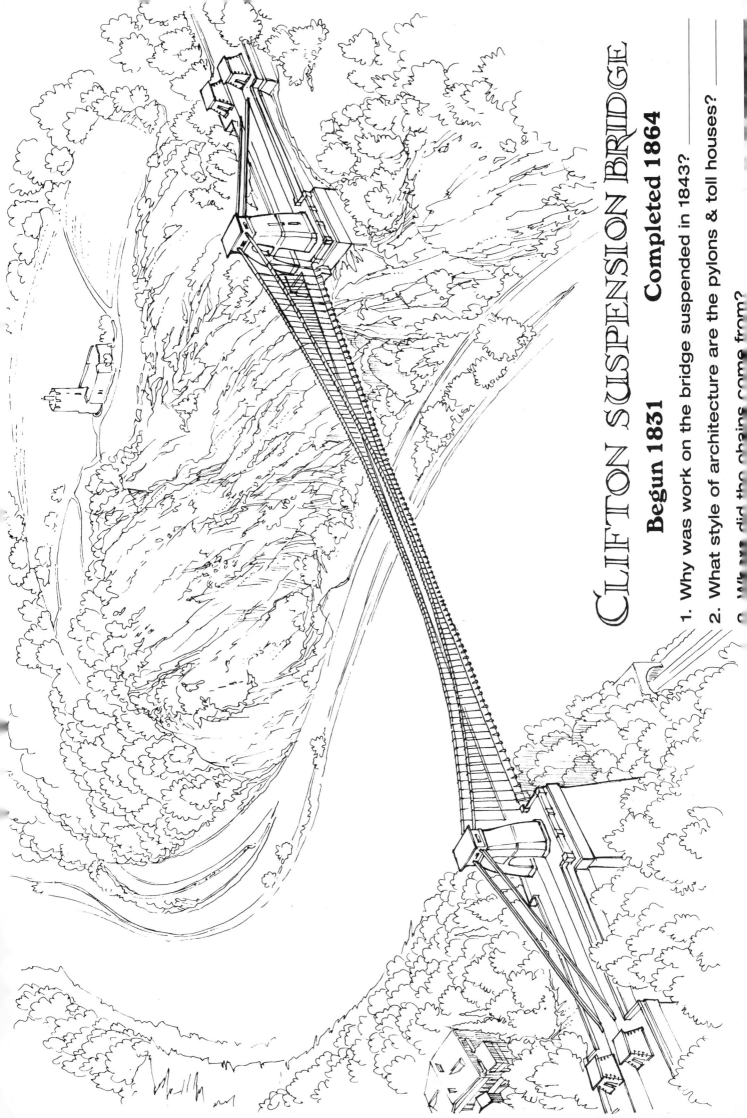

CLIFTON SUSPENSION BRIDGE

Begun 1831   Completed 1864

1. Why was work on the bridge suspended in 1843?

2. What style of architecture are the pylons & toll houses?

3. Where did the chains come from?

THE ROYAL WESTERN HOTEL

ENGLAND'S FIRST MODERN HOTEL DESIGNED BY R.S.POPE & I.K.BRUNEL 1837

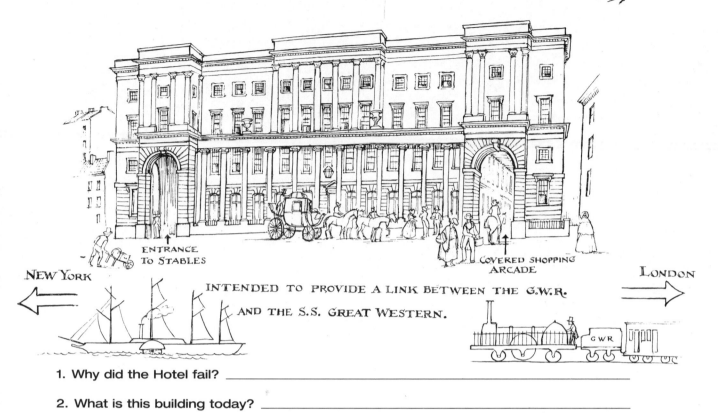

ENTRANCE TO STABLES

COVERED SHOPPING ARCADE

NEW YORK ←

INTENDED TO PROVIDE A LINK BETWEEN THE G.W.R. AND THE S.S. GREAT WESTERN.

LONDON →

1. Why did the Hotel fail? _____

2. What is this building today? _____

THE GREAT WESTERN RAILWAY
1833 - 1841

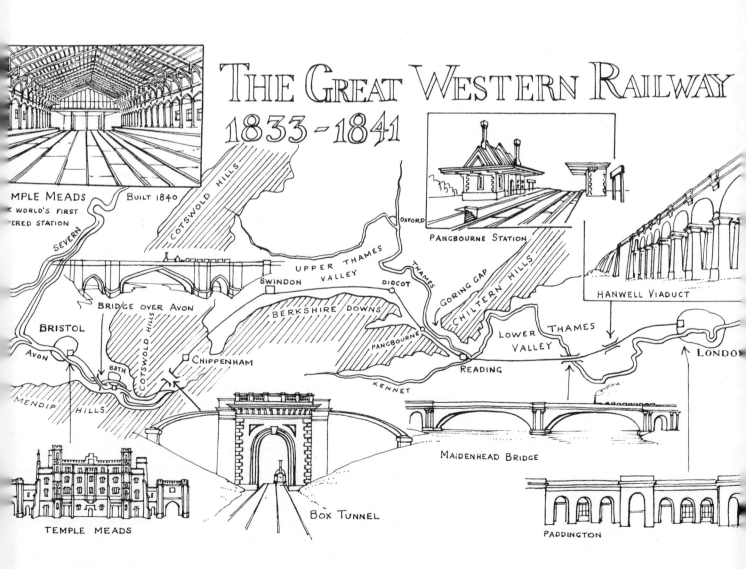

TEMPLE MEADS
THE WORLD'S FIRST COVERED STATION
BUILT 1840

COTSWOLD HILLS

OXFORD

PANGBOURNE STATION

HANWELL VIADUCT

SEVERN

UPPER THAMES VALLEY

SWINDON

DIDCOT

THAMES

GORING GAP

CHILTERN HILLS

LOWER THAMES VALLEY

LONDON

BRIDGE OVER AVON

BERKSHIRE DOWNS

PANGBOURNE

BRISTOL

AVON

BATH

COTSWOLD HILLS

CHIPPENHAM

READING

KENNET

MENDIP HILLS

BOX TUNNEL

MAIDENHEAD BRIDGE

TEMPLE MEADS

PADDINGTON

TEMPLE MEADS

THE WORLD'S FIRST
COMPREHENSIVE
RAILWAY TERMINUS

OPENED 1841

T _____
S _____

ARR _____

1st CLASS B O _____

2nd CLASS B _____

DEP _____

C S _____

6. Where did 3rd Class passengers board the train?

_____

_____

T _____

E D O _____

W T _____

O _____

1. Why is it called Temple Meads?

_____
_____
_____

2. In what style of Architecture is it built? _____

3. In what ways was it the world's first comprehensive railway station?

_____
_____
_____
_____
_____
_____

4. What is remarkable about the roof?

_____
_____

5. Why has most of it survived intact?

Label: TRAIN SHED. CARRIAG
SHED. TUNNEL. WATER TOWE
ARRIVALS. DEPARTURES.
1st. CLASS BOOKING OFFICE.
2nd. BOOKING OFFICE.
OFFICES OF G.W.R. COMPANY.
BOARD ROOM FOR MEETING OF
DIRECTORS. ENGINEERS'
DRAWING OFFICE.

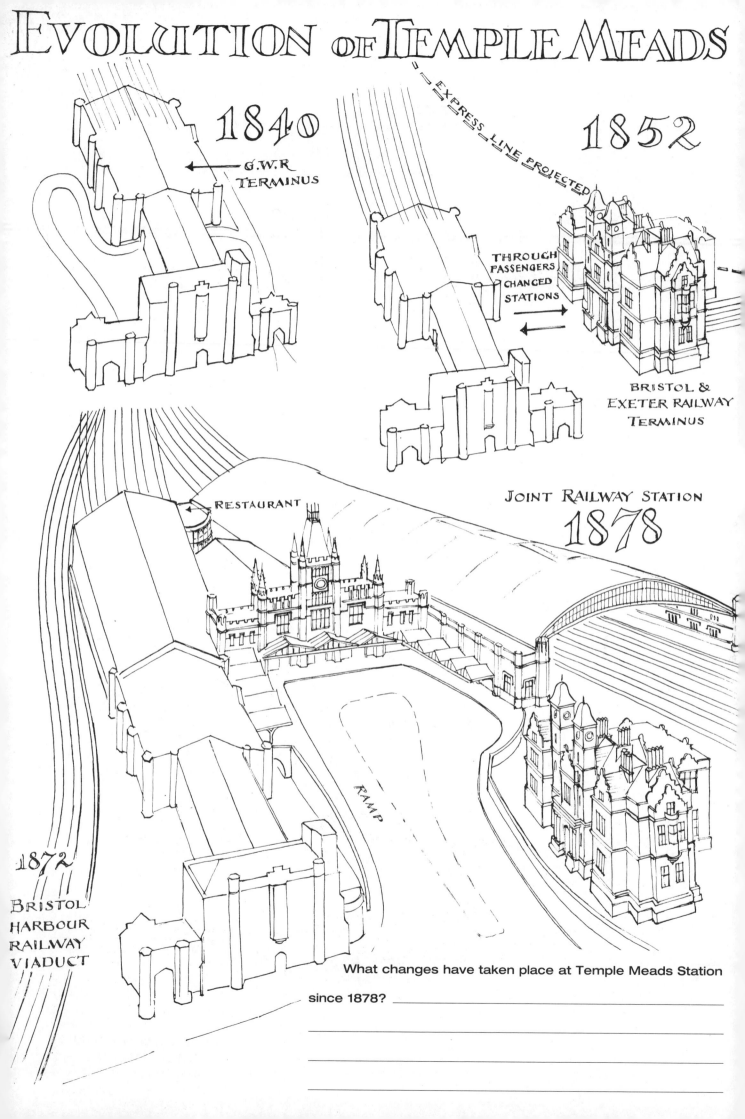

EVOLUTION OF TEMPLE MEADS

1840
← G.W.R TERMINUS

1852
EXPRESS LINE PROJECTED
THROUGH PASSENGERS CHANGED STATIONS
BRISTOL & EXETER RAILWAY TERMINUS

JOINT RAILWAY STATION
1878
RESTAURANT

1872 BRISTOL HARBOUR RAILWAY VIADUCT

RAMP

What changes have taken place at Temple Meads Station since 1878? _____

THE
S.S. GREAT BRITAIN

SS GREAT BRITAIN

S.S. Great Britain 1843

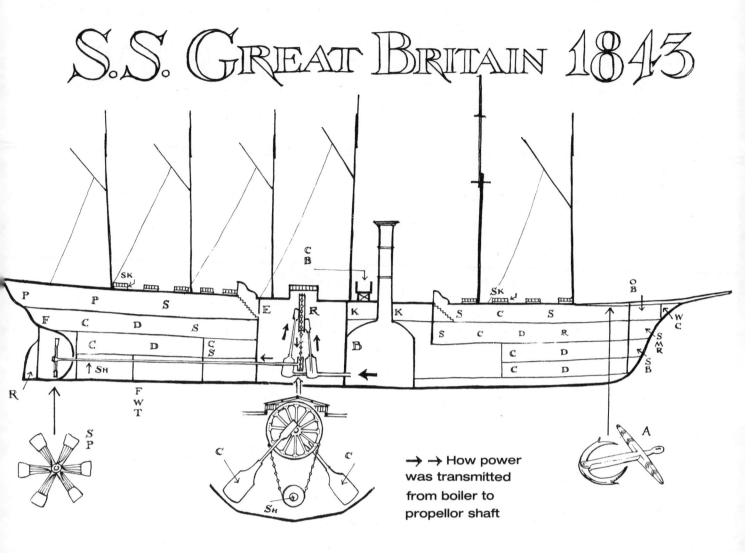

→ → How power was transmitted from boiler to propellor shaft

LABEL: CAPTAIN'S BRIDGE.

PRINCIPAL PROMENADE SALOON 110′ x 48′ with 24 single berths on each side.

FIRST CLASS DINING SALOON 100′ x 50′.   SKYLIGHTS.

CARGO DECK.   COAL STORE.

FRESH WATER TANK.

ENGINE ROOM.   CYLINDERS.   SHAFT.

KITCHENS.   BOILER.

SECOND-CLASS SALOON 40 bed places on each side.

OFFICERS' BERTHS.   WATER CLOSETS.   SECOND CLASS DINING ROOM.

SAILORS' MESS ROOM.   SAILORS' BERTHS.

ANCHOR.

SCREW PROPELLOR.   RUDDER.

PASSENGER ACCOMMODATION
ON BOARD THE S.S. GREAT BRITAIN
1842

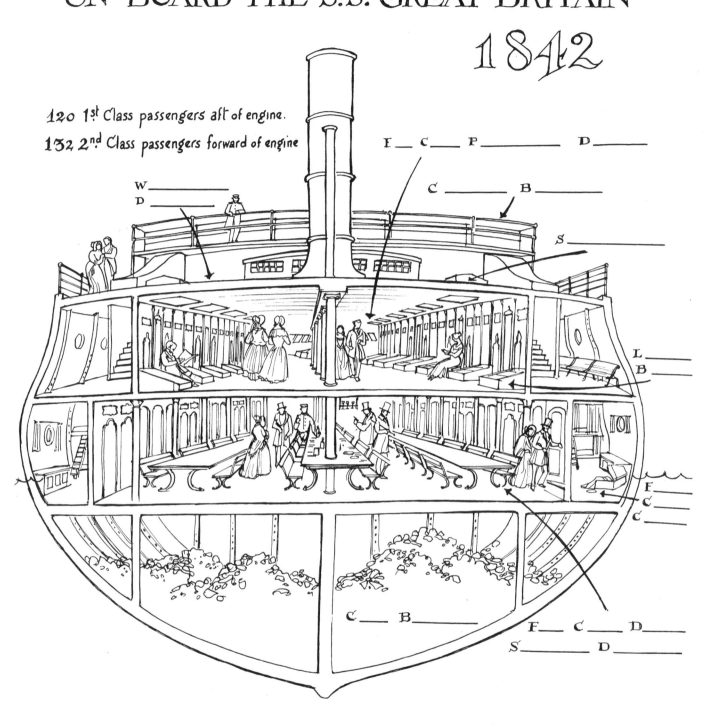

120 1st Class passengers aft of engine.

132 2nd Class passengers forward of engine

W _____

D _____

F __ C __ P _____ D _____

C _____ B _____

S _____

L _____

B _____

F

C

C

C __ B _____

F __ C __ D _____

S _____ D _____

Label: WEATHER DECK. CAPTAIN'S BRIDGE. SKYLIGHT. FIRST CLASS PROMENADE DECK.

FIRST CLASS DINING SALOON DECK. FIRST CLASS CABIN. LIGHT BOX. COAL BUNKER.

1. How was the Dining Saloon lit? _____

_____

2. How was passenger accommodation altered in 1852? _____

_____

ASHTON COURT WHO BUILT WHAT?

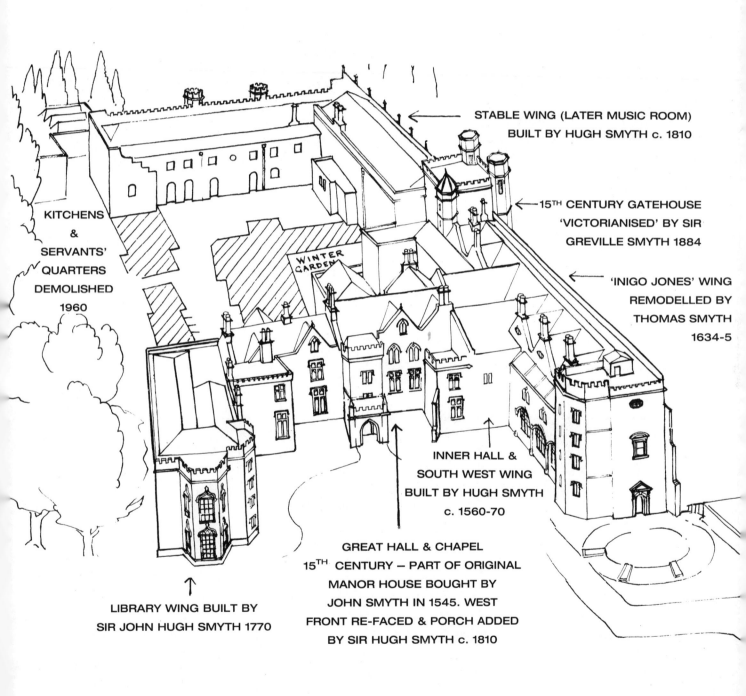

STABLE WING (LATER MUSIC ROOM)
BUILT BY HUGH SMYTH c. 1810

15TH CENTURY GATEHOUSE
'VICTORIANISED' BY SIR
GREVILLE SMYTH 1884

'INIGO JONES' WING
REMODELLED BY
THOMAS SMYTH
1634-5

KITCHENS
&
SERVANTS'
QUARTERS
DEMOLISHED
1960

WINTER GARDEN

INNER HALL &
SOUTH WEST WING
BUILT BY HUGH SMYTH
c. 1560-70

GREAT HALL & CHAPEL
15TH CENTURY — PART OF ORIGINAL
MANOR HOUSE BOUGHT BY
JOHN SMYTH IN 1545. WEST
FRONT RE-FACED & PORCH ADDED
BY SIR HUGH SMYTH c. 1810

LIBRARY WING BUILT BY
SIR JOHN HUGH SMYTH 1770

THE HOUSEHOLD OF SIR

ABOVE STAIRS

ASHTON 1853

Sir Greville courted Emily for 27 years before she was free to marry him.

Emily was "the loveliest woman in the West of England". It was even rumoured that the Prince of Wales was her lover...

Dr. Holman – Greville's resident physician and companion when big-game hunting in Africa & India.

Thomas Jeans – Greville's old tutor.
A frequent visitor to Ashton Court.

Greville's Mother Eliza Upton lived at Ashton Court until her death in 1870.

Greville's Aunt Louisa Prior who kept house for him after his mother died.

Esmé – Greville's daughter by Emily when she was still married to George Oldham Edwards, Banker of Redland Cou

She married in 1890 the Hon. Gilbert Irby & inherited the Smyth Estate in 1914.

Greville's courier Frederick Brown. He spent six months of every year travelling.

George Eyton, Greville's valet.

Nanny Bowers with Esmé's daughter Sylvia. She was later nanny to Sylvia's children & ended her days in the Almshouses built by Emily in Long Ashton.

Agnes Watson, Emily's lady's maid. She left her former mistress (Greville's sister) because she got fed up packing & unpacking suitcases (58 hotels a year). She then married Greville's courier Brown!

Esmé's governess Mrs. Knightly-Cox whom she nicknamed "Hoppity". In old age she lived at Ashton Court.

GREVILLE SMYTH BART.
COURT 1901
BELOW STAIRS

Hannah Emery, House keeper.

William Curtis, Butler.

Helen Maynard, Chamber maid.

Louisa Pereden, Cook.

George Lloyd, First Footman. The footmen did not stay long so the first was always called William & the second James to avoid confusion.

Sarah Wells, Kitchen maid.

George Liston, 2nd footman. They wore canary coloured stockings, black & canary coats & breeches, red waistcoats with a white stripe.

Agnes Rawlinson, Parlour maid.

Henry Saunders, Coachman.

Ann Thomas, Scullery maid.

John Wilkinson, Hall-boy.

Thomas Fry, Park-keeper.

James Reith, Head-gardener.

Joseph Millear, Gardener's boy.

Arthur Speed, Stable-boy.

William Watts, Groom.

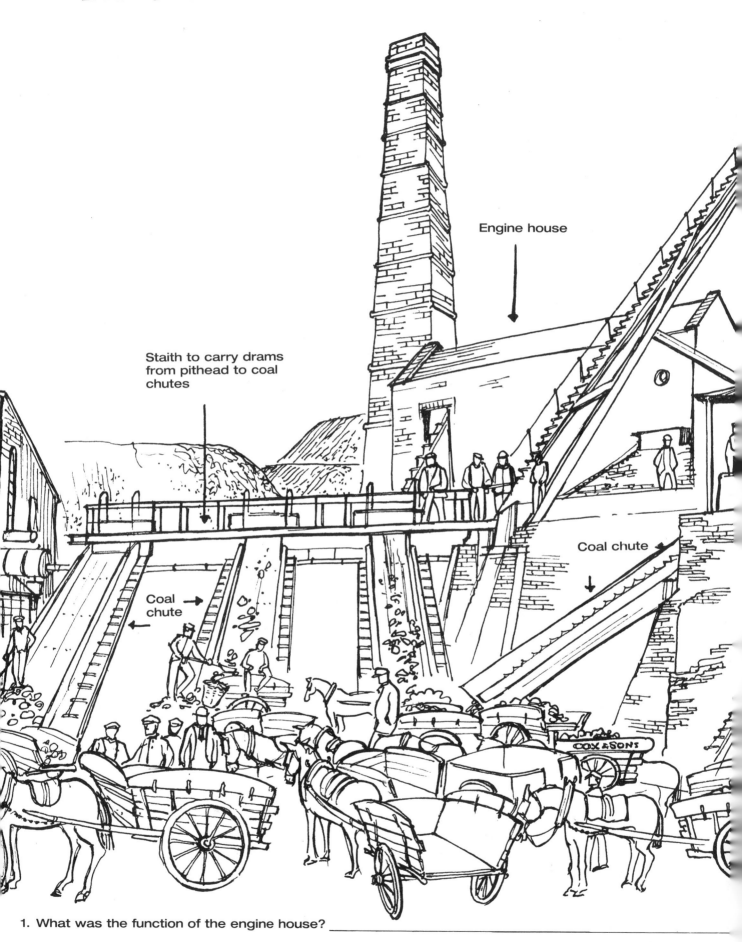

Engine house

Staith to carry drams from pithead to coal chutes

Coal chute

Coal chute

COX & SONS

1. What was the function of the engine house? _____

2. How was coal conveyed from the pit-head to the waiting carts? _____

3. What is happening in the foreground? _____

4. What occupies this site today? _____

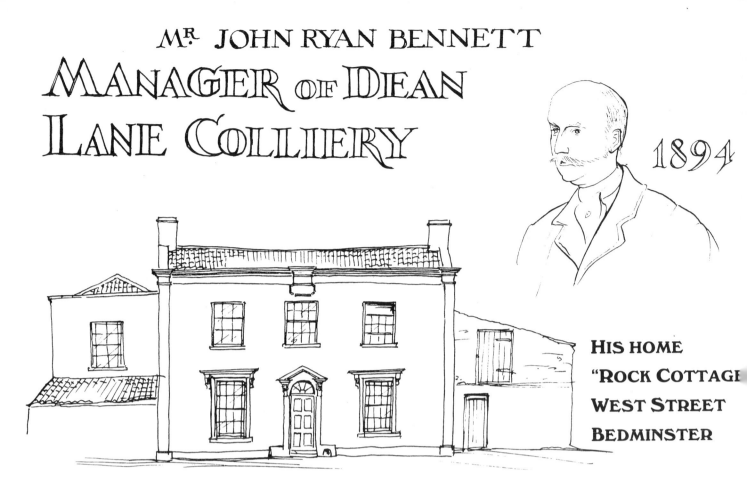

MR. JOHN RYAN BENNETT
MANAGER OF DEAN LANE COLLIERY

1894

**HIS HOME
"ROCK COTTAGE
WEST STREET
BEDMINSTER**

HIS DAUGHTERS: Constance, Margery, Rachel, Dorothy and Evelyn.

In the centre is his son Henry. One afternoon the baby was tiresome — so his nursemaid took him down the orchard at the back of the house so that his sisters were not disturbed during their lessons with the governess. At the bottom of the orchard was a well. The nursemaid sat on the parapet with Henry in her lap, but the parapet was crumbling and collapsed and both nursemaid and baby fell down the well. Half way down a rusty pipe impaled her side and checked her fall but her cries for help were not heard for over an hour. During the whole time she did not let go of Henry. Both were rescued and recovered. The housemaid later married the gardener, but sad to say Henry was killed in the First World War.

Miner's Cottage 1899

COAL HOUSE

EARTH CLOSET

PIG OR CHICKENS

SCULLERY

PUMP SHARED BY SEVERAL HOUSEHOLDS

STOVE

STAIRS TO 3 BEDROOMS

KITCHEN

HOUSE NEXT DOOR

FIRE

PARLOUR

PARAFFIN LAMP

① **NO ELECTRIC POWER**
   – candles
   – paraffin lamps

② **NO RUNNING WATER**
   – All water fetched from pump

③ **NO MAIN SEWER**
   – earth closet
   – cesspool emptied periodically

④ **NO BATHROOM** Miners scrubbed by wives in tin bath in front of kitchen fire.

EARTH CLOSET (outdoors)
   – No light
   – No flush

MINERS' COTTAGES

FOOT OF BEDMINSTER DOWN

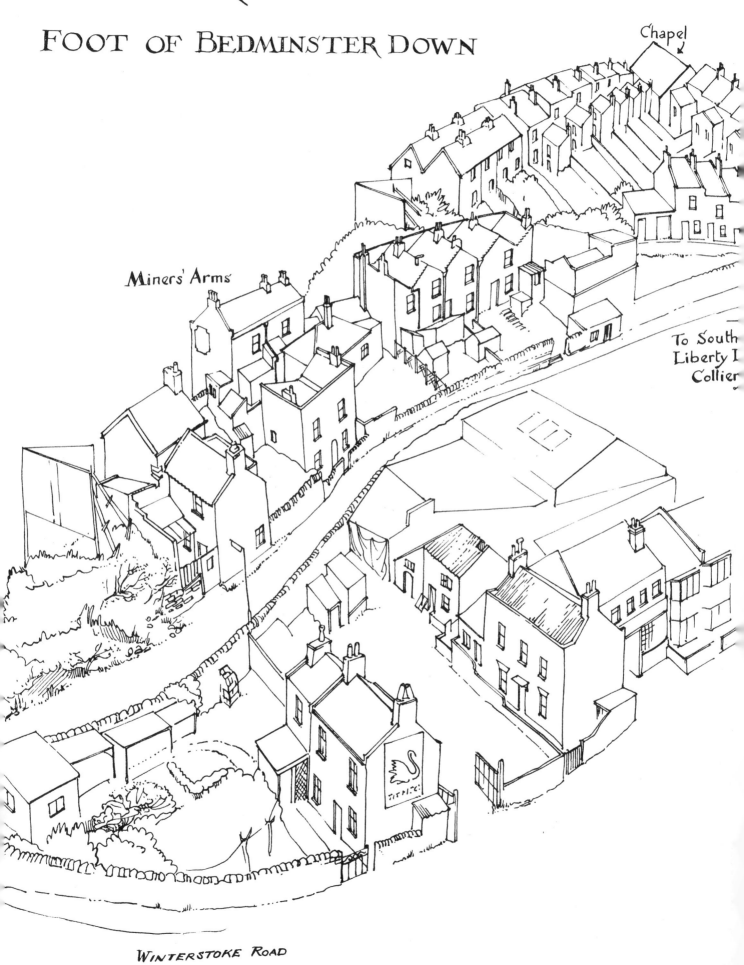

Chapel

Miners' Arms

To South
Liberty I
Collier

WINTERSTOKE ROAD

Observatory

Hot Wells Spa 1860

Pylon of Clifton Suspension Bridge — begun 1831
completed 1864.

COLONNADE of
Shops — now
private dwelling houses.

T BOLTON BRIDGE

CLIFTON & BATHS

BRISTOL HOT WELLS

TEPID SWIMMING BATH OPEN SUMMER AND WINTER

WELLS HOUSE
nolished in 1862
construction of
tway

HOT, COLD, SHOWER, DOUCHE & ALL OTHER BATHS ALWAYS OPEN

Horse Bus   1880

Long Ashton ~ Bristol

Horse Tram
1872

Upper Maudlin Street ~ Whiteladies Road

All tram services were electrified in 1900 and continued to operate until 1940.

ANSWERS

Page

2–3 St. Augustine's the Less, Bristol Cathedral, St. Mark's (Lord Mayor's Chapel) and St. Michael's.

4 The Old Vic, Princess Victoria Street, Victoria Rooms, Victoria Square.

5 1. Greek (Corinthian). 2. Edward VII. 3. College Green. 4. Boer War 1899-1902. 5. On a traffic island in front of the Victoria Rooms.

6–7 1843 Guildhall, Broad Street. Neo-Gothic.

1847 Queen Elizabeth's Hospital, Brandon Hill. Tudor.

1857 Academy of Fine Art, now Royal West of England Academy. Italian Renaissance. Flights of steps removed.

1858 West of England & South Wales Bank (now Lloyds), Corn Street. Italian Renaissance. Additional bay added on the left and entrance moved from centre to new bay.

1866 Former Museum & Library (now University refectory), Queens Road. Italian Gothic. Pinnacles and many details destroyed in World War Two.

1867 Colston Hall. Byzantine.

1871 Granary. Bristol Byzantine.

1894 E. Shed, Watershed. Jacobean.

8 1. The Bishop of Bristol and Recorder of the City had voted against the great Reform Bill which planned to give the vote to more people.

2. i. Lord Mayor's Mansion House. ii. Customs House. iii. Two sides of Queen Square. iv. Bishop's Palace. v. New Gaol. vi. Toll House. vii. Bridewell. viii. Lawford's Gate Prison.

10 1. On Cumberland Road overlooking the New Cut.

2. Prisoners were classified and segregated according to their crime. Separate cells for criminal cases. Cells were centrally heated. A chapel was built by the prisoners from the proceeds of their labour.

3. The entrance gate and part of the surrounding wall.

12 Outside the Bristol & West Building Society extension, Broad Quay.

14 1. Funds ran out. 2. Egyptian. 3. Hungerford Footbridge over the Thames, also built by Brunel but demolished in 1860.

15 1. Brunel failed to get support for his plan to extend the GWR to the dockside and the hotel remained in a backwater and closed by 1855.

2. Brunel House; home of the City Planning Dept.

16 1. The Meads (or meadows) belonged to the Parish of the Temple Church.

2. Tudor Gothic.

3. It incorporated platforms, ticket offices, boardrooms, carriage shed etc. all under the same roof.

4. It is a wooden hammer-beam roof with a span of 72 feet.

5. It became obsolete after the construction of the joint station in 1878.

6. Some distance up the track and well outside the station.

17 The broad gauge was replaced by standard gauge by 1898. The GWR and Bristol & Exeter termini became redundant. Pointed roof of clock tower destroyed in World War Two. There are now many more additional lines and a platform east of the roof span.
Bristol Harbour railway discontinued.

20 1. From light boxes in the promenade deck above — which were directly underneath skylights on the weather deck.

2. Additional first class quarters added above promenade deck. Two funnels side by side and much more canvas (sailpower).

24–25 1. To provide power to raise the cages up the shafts.

2. Drams ran from the cage down a gradual incline and tipped the coal down chutes.

3. Hauliers are waiting their turn to collect coal from the chutes or making their way to the weighbridge, and so to the factories and railways which relied on coal; or to the docks for export.

4. Dean Lane playground and skate-board park.